My Day by Day

Daily Planner
and Journal

Activinotes

Activinotes

DAILY JOURNALS, PLANNERS, NOTEBOOKS AND OTHER BLANK BOOKS

Time	Monday	Tuesday	Wednesday	Thursday	Friday
6:00 AM					
7:00 AM					
8:00 AM					
9:00 AM					
10:00 AM					
11:00 AM					
12:00 NN					
1:00 PM					
2:00 PM					
3:00 PM					
4:00 PM					
5:00 PM					

notes:
_____
_____
_____
_____
_____

Time	Monday	Tuesday	Wednesday	Thursday	Friday
6:00 AM					
7:00 AM					
8:00 AM					
9:00 AM					
10:00 AM					
11:00 AM					
12:00 NN					
1:00 PM					
2:00 PM					
3:00 PM					
4:00 PM					
5:00 PM					

notes:

Time	Monday	Tuesday	Wednesday	**Thursday**	Friday
6:00 AM					
7:00 AM					
8:00 AM					
9:00 AM					
10:00 AM					
11:00 AM					
12:00 NN					
1:00 PM					
2:00 PM					
3:00 PM					
4:00 PM					
5:00 PM					

notes:

Time	Monday	Tuesday	Wednesday	Thursday	Friday
6:00 AM					
7:00 AM					
8:00 AM					
9:00 AM					
10:00 AM					
11:00 AM					
12:00 NN					
1:00 PM					
2:00 PM					
3:00 PM					
4:00 PM					
5:00 PM					

notes:
_____
_____
_____
_____
_____
_____

Time	Monday	Tuesday	Wednesday	**Thursday**	Friday
6:00 AM					
7:00 AM					
8:00 AM					
9:00 AM					
10:00 AM					
11:00 AM					
12:00 NN					
1:00 PM					
2:00 PM					
3:00 PM					
4:00 PM					
5:00 PM					

notes:

Time	Monday	Tuesday	Wednesday	Thursday	Friday
6:00 AM					
7:00 AM					
8:00 AM					
9:00 AM					
10:00 AM					
11:00 AM					
12:00 NN					
1:00 PM					
2:00 PM					
3:00 PM					
4:00 PM					
5:00 PM					

notes:

Time	Monday	Tuesday	Wednesday	**Thursday**	Friday
6:00 AM					
7:00 AM					
8:00 AM					
9:00 AM					
10:00 AM					
11:00 AM					
12:00 NN					
1:00 PM					
2:00 PM					
3:00 PM					
4:00 PM					
5:00 PM					

notes:

Time	Monday	Tuesday	Wednesday	Thursday	Friday
6:00 AM					
7:00 AM					
8:00 AM					
9:00 AM					
10:00 AM					
11:00 AM					
12:00 NN					
1:00 PM					
2:00 PM					
3:00 PM					
4:00 PM					
5:00 PM					

notes:

Time	Monday	Tuesday	Wednesday	Thursday	Friday
6:00 AM					
7:00 AM					
8:00 AM					
9:00 AM					
10:00 AM					
11:00 AM					
12:00 NN					
1:00 PM					
2:00 PM					
3:00 PM					
4:00 PM					
5:00 PM					

notes:

Time	Monday	Tuesday	Wednesday	Thursday	Friday
6:00 AM					
7:00 AM					
8:00 AM					
9:00 AM					
10:00 AM					
11:00 AM					
12:00 NN					
1:00 PM					
2:00 PM					
3:00 PM					
4:00 PM					
5:00 PM					

notes:

Time	Monday	Tuesday	Wednesday	Thursday	Friday
6:00 AM					
7:00 AM					
8:00 AM					
9:00 AM					
10:00 AM					
11:00 AM					
12:00 NN					
1:00 PM					
2:00 PM					
3:00 PM					
4:00 PM					
5:00 PM					

notes:

Time	Monday	Tuesday	Wednesday	Thursday	Friday
6:00 AM					
7:00 AM					
8:00 AM					
9:00 AM					
10:00 AM					
11:00 AM					
12:00 NN					
1:00 PM					
2:00 PM					
3:00 PM					
4:00 PM					
5:00 PM					

notes:
_____
_____
_____
_____
_____

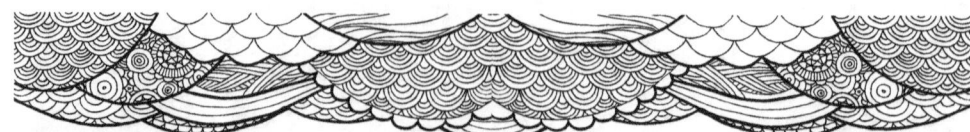

Time	Monday	Tuesday	Wednesday	Thursday	Friday
6:00 AM					
7:00 AM					
8:00 AM					
9:00 AM					
10:00 AM					
11:00 AM					
12:00 NN					
1:00 PM					
2:00 PM					
3:00 PM					
4:00 PM					
5:00 PM					

notes:
_____
_____
_____
_____
_____

Time	Monday	Tuesday	Wednesday	**Thursday**	Friday
6:00 AM					
7:00 AM					
8:00 AM					
9:00 AM					
10:00 AM					
11:00 AM					
12:00 NN					
1:00 PM					
2:00 PM					
3:00 PM					
4:00 PM					
5:00 PM					

notes:

_____

_____

_____

_____

_____

Time	Monday	Tuesday	Wednesday	**Thursday**	Friday
6:00 AM					
7:00 AM					
8:00 AM					
9:00 AM					
10:00 AM					
11:00 AM					
12:00 NN					
1:00 PM					
2:00 PM					
3:00 PM					
4:00 PM					
5:00 PM					

notes:

Time	Monday	Tuesday	Wednesday	Thursday	Friday
6:00 AM					
7:00 AM					
8:00 AM					
9:00 AM					
10:00 AM					
11:00 AM					
12:00 NN					
1:00 PM					
2:00 PM					
3:00 PM					
4:00 PM					
5:00 PM					

notes:

Time	Monday	Tuesday	Wednesday	Thursday	Friday
6:00 AM					
7:00 AM					
8:00 AM					
9:00 AM					
10:00 AM					
11:00 AM					
12:00 NN					
1:00 PM					
2:00 PM					
3:00 PM					
4:00 PM					
5:00 PM					

notes:
_____
_____
_____
_____

Time	Monday	Tuesday	Wednesday	Thursday	Friday
6:00 AM					
7:00 AM					
8:00 AM					
9:00 AM					
10:00 AM					
11:00 AM					
12:00 NN					
1:00 PM					
2:00 PM					
3:00 PM					
4:00 PM					
5:00 PM					

notes:

Time	Monday	Tuesday	Wednesday	**Thursday**	Friday
6:00 AM					
7:00 AM					
8:00 AM					
9:00 AM					
10:00 AM					
11:00 AM					
12:00 NN					
1:00 PM					
2:00 PM					
3:00 PM					
4:00 PM					
5:00 PM					

notes:

Time	Monday	Tuesday	Wednesday	**Thursday**	Friday
6:00 AM					
7:00 AM					
8:00 AM					
9:00 AM					
10:00 AM					
11:00 AM					
12:00 NN					
1:00 PM					
2:00 PM					
3:00 PM					
4:00 PM					
5:00 PM					

notes:

_____

_____

_____

_____

_____

Time	Monday	Tuesday	Wednesday	Thursday	Friday
6:00 AM					
7:00 AM					
8:00 AM					
9:00 AM					
10:00 AM					
11:00 AM					
12:00 NN					
1:00 PM					
2:00 PM					
3:00 PM					
4:00 PM					
5:00 PM					

notes:

Time	Monday	Tuesday	Wednesday	**Thursday**	Friday
6:00 AM					
7:00 AM					
8:00 AM					
9:00 AM					
10:00 AM					
11:00 AM					
12:00 NN					
1:00 PM					
2:00 PM					
3:00 PM					
4:00 PM					
5:00 PM					

notes:
_____
_____
_____
_____
_____

Time	Monday	Tuesday	Wednesday	**Thursday**	Friday
6:00 AM					
7:00 AM					
8:00 AM					
9:00 AM					
10:00 AM					
11:00 AM					
12:00 NN					
1:00 PM					
2:00 PM					
3:00 PM					
4:00 PM					
5:00 PM					

notes:

Time	Monday	Tuesday	Wednesday	Thursday	Friday
6:00 AM					
7:00 AM					
8:00 AM					
9:00 AM					
10:00 AM					
11:00 AM					
12:00 NN					
1:00 PM					
2:00 PM					
3:00 PM					
4:00 PM					
5:00 PM					

notes:

_____

_____

_____

_____

_____

Time	Monday	Tuesday	Wednesday	Thursday	Friday
6:00 AM					
7:00 AM					
8:00 AM					
9:00 AM					
10:00 AM					
11:00 AM					
12:00 NN					
1:00 PM					
2:00 PM					
3:00 PM					
4:00 PM					
5:00 PM					

notes:

Time	Monday	Tuesday	Wednesday	**Thursday**	Friday
6:00 AM					
7:00 AM					
8:00 AM					
9:00 AM					
10:00 AM					
11:00 AM					
12:00 NN					
1:00 PM					
2:00 PM					
3:00 PM					
4:00 PM					
5:00 PM					

notes:

Time	Monday	Tuesday	Wednesday	**Thursday**	Friday
6:00 AM					
7:00 AM					
8:00 AM					
9:00 AM					
10:00 AM					
11:00 AM					
12:00 NN					
1:00 PM					
2:00 PM					
3:00 PM					
4:00 PM					
5:00 PM					

notes:

Time	Monday	Tuesday	Wednesday	Thursday	Friday
6:00 AM					
7:00 AM					
8:00 AM					
9:00 AM					
10:00 AM					
11:00 AM					
12:00 NN					
1:00 PM					
2:00 PM					
3:00 PM					
4:00 PM					
5:00 PM					

notes:

Time	Monday	Tuesday	Wednesday	Thursday	Friday
6:00 AM					
7:00 AM					
8:00 AM					
9:00 AM					
10:00 AM					
11:00 AM					
12:00 NN					
1:00 PM					
2:00 PM					
3:00 PM					
4:00 PM					
5:00 PM					

notes:

Time	Monday	Tuesday	Wednesday	Thursday	Friday
6:00 AM					
7:00 AM					
8:00 AM					
9:00 AM					
10:00 AM					
11:00 AM					
12:00 NN					
1:00 PM					
2:00 PM					
3:00 PM					
4:00 PM					
5:00 PM					

notes:

Time	Monday	Tuesday	Wednesday	Thursday	Friday
6:00 AM					
7:00 AM					
8:00 AM					
9:00 AM					
10:00 AM					
11:00 AM					
12:00 NN					
1:00 PM					
2:00 PM					
3:00 PM					
4:00 PM					
5:00 PM					

notes:

Time	Monday	Tuesday	Wednesday	Thursday	Friday
6:00 AM					
7:00 AM					
8:00 AM					
9:00 AM					
10:00 AM					
11:00 AM					
12:00 NN					
1:00 PM					
2:00 PM					
3:00 PM					
4:00 PM					
5:00 PM					

notes:

Time	Monday	Tuesday	Wednesday	Thursday	Friday
6:00 AM					
7:00 AM					
8:00 AM					
9:00 AM					
10:00 AM					
11:00 AM					
12:00 NN					
1:00 PM					
2:00 PM					
3:00 PM					
4:00 PM					
5:00 PM					

notes:

Time	Monday	Tuesday	Wednesday	Thursday	Friday
6:00 AM					
7:00 AM					
8:00 AM					
9:00 AM					
10:00 AM					
11:00 AM					
12:00 NN					
1:00 PM					
2:00 PM					
3:00 PM					
4:00 PM					
5:00 PM					

notes:

Time	Monday	Tuesday	Wednesday	Thursday	Friday
6:00 AM					
7:00 AM					
8:00 AM					
9:00 AM					
10:00 AM					
11:00 AM					
12:00 NN					
1:00 PM					
2:00 PM					
3:00 PM					
4:00 PM					
5:00 PM					

notes:

Time	Monday	Tuesday	Wednesday	Thursday	Friday
6:00 AM					
7:00 AM					
8:00 AM					
9:00 AM					
10:00 AM					
11:00 AM					
12:00 NN					
1:00 PM					
2:00 PM					
3:00 PM					
4:00 PM					
5:00 PM					

notes:

Time	Monday	Tuesday	Wednesday	Thursday	Friday
6:00 AM					
7:00 AM					
8:00 AM					
9:00 AM					
10:00 AM					
11:00 AM					
12:00 NN					
1:00 PM					
2:00 PM					
3:00 PM					
4:00 PM					
5:00 PM					

notes:
_____
_____
_____
_____
_____

Time	Monday	Tuesday	Wednesday	**Thursday**	Friday
6:00 AM					
7:00 AM					
8:00 AM					
9:00 AM					
10:00 AM					
11:00 AM					
12:00 NN					
1:00 PM					
2:00 PM					
3:00 PM					
4:00 PM					
5:00 PM					

notes:

Time	Monday	Tuesday	Wednesday	Thursday	Friday
6:00 AM					
7:00 AM					
8:00 AM					
9:00 AM					
10:00 AM					
11:00 AM					
12:00 NN					
1:00 PM					
2:00 PM					
3:00 PM					
4:00 PM					
5:00 PM					

notes:

Time	Monday	Tuesday	Wednesday	Thursday	Friday
6:00 AM					
7:00 AM					
8:00 AM					
9:00 AM					
10:00 AM					
11:00 AM					
12:00 NN					
1:00 PM					
2:00 PM					
3:00 PM					
4:00 PM					
5:00 PM					

notes:

Time	Monday	Tuesday	Wednesday	Thursday	Friday
6:00 AM					
7:00 AM					
8:00 AM					
9:00 AM					
10:00 AM					
11:00 AM					
12:00 NN					
1:00 PM					
2:00 PM					
3:00 PM					
4:00 PM					
5:00 PM					

notes:
_____
_____
_____
_____
_____

Time	Monday	Tuesday	Wednesday	Thursday	Friday
6:00 AM					
7:00 AM					
8:00 AM					
9:00 AM					
10:00 AM					
11:00 AM					
12:00 NN					
1:00 PM					
2:00 PM					
3:00 PM					
4:00 PM					
5:00 PM					

notes:
_____
_____
_____
_____
_____

Time	Monday	Tuesday	Wednesday	**Thursday**	Friday
6:00 AM					
7:00 AM					
8:00 AM					
9:00 AM					
10:00 AM					
11:00 AM					
12:00 NN					
1:00 PM					
2:00 PM					
3:00 PM					
4:00 PM					
5:00 PM					

notes:

Time	Monday	Tuesday	Wednesday	Thursday	Friday
6:00 AM					
7:00 AM					
8:00 AM					
9:00 AM					
10:00 AM					
11:00 AM					
12:00 NN					
1:00 PM					
2:00 PM					
3:00 PM					
4:00 PM					
5:00 PM					

notes:
_____
_____
_____
_____
_____

Time	Monday	Tuesday	Wednesday	Thursday	Friday
6:00 AM					
7:00 AM					
8:00 AM					
9:00 AM					
10:00 AM					
11:00 AM					
12:00 NN					
1:00 PM					
2:00 PM					
3:00 PM					
4:00 PM					
5:00 PM					

notes:

Time	Monday	Tuesday	Wednesday	Thursday	Friday
6:00 AM					
7:00 AM					
8:00 AM					
9:00 AM					
10:00 AM					
11:00 AM					
12:00 NN					
1:00 PM					
2:00 PM					
3:00 PM					
4:00 PM					
5:00 PM					

notes:

Time	Monday	Tuesday	Wednesday	Thursday	Friday
6:00 AM					
7:00 AM					
8:00 AM					
9:00 AM					
10:00 AM					
11:00 AM					
12:00 NN					
1:00 PM					
2:00 PM					
3:00 PM					
4:00 PM					
5:00 PM					

notes:
_____
_____
_____
_____
_____

Time	Monday	Tuesday	Wednesday	Thursday	Friday
6:00 AM					
7:00 AM					
8:00 AM					
9:00 AM					
10:00 AM					
11:00 AM					
12:00 NN					
1:00 PM					
2:00 PM					
3:00 PM					
4:00 PM					
5:00 PM					

notes:

Time	Monday	Tuesday	Wednesday	Thursday	Friday
6:00 AM					
7:00 AM					
8:00 AM					
9:00 AM					
10:00 AM					
11:00 AM					
12:00 NN					
1:00 PM					
2:00 PM					
3:00 PM					
4:00 PM					
5:00 PM					

notes:

Time	Monday	Tuesday	Wednesday	Thursday	Friday
6:00 AM					
7:00 AM					
8:00 AM					
9:00 AM					
10:00 AM					
11:00 AM					
12:00 NN					
1:00 PM					
2:00 PM					
3:00 PM					
4:00 PM					
5:00 PM					

notes:
_____
_____
_____
_____
_____

Time	Monday	Tuesday	Wednesday	**Thursday**	Friday
6:00 AM					
7:00 AM					
8:00 AM					
9:00 AM					
10:00 AM					
11:00 AM					
12:00 NN					
1:00 PM					
2:00 PM					
3:00 PM					
4:00 PM					
5:00 PM					

notes:

Time	Monday	Tuesday	Wednesday	Thursday	Friday
6:00 AM					
7:00 AM					
8:00 AM					
9:00 AM					
10:00 AM					
11:00 AM					
12:00 NN					
1:00 PM					
2:00 PM					
3:00 PM					
4:00 PM					
5:00 PM					

notes:

Time	Monday	Tuesday	Wednesday	Thursday	Friday
6:00 AM					
7:00 AM					
8:00 AM					
9:00 AM					
10:00 AM					
11:00 AM					
12:00 NN					
1:00 PM					
2:00 PM					
3:00 PM					
4:00 PM					
5:00 PM					

notes:

Time	Monday	Tuesday	Wednesday	Thursday	Friday
6:00 AM					
7:00 AM					
8:00 AM					
9:00 AM					
10:00 AM					
11:00 AM					
12:00 NN					
1:00 PM					
2:00 PM					
3:00 PM					
4:00 PM					
5:00 PM					

notes:
_____
_____
_____
_____
_____

Time	Monday	Tuesday	Wednesday	Thursday	Friday
6:00 AM					
7:00 AM					
8:00 AM					
9:00 AM					
10:00 AM					
11:00 AM					
12:00 NN					
1:00 PM					
2:00 PM					
3:00 PM					
4:00 PM					
5:00 PM					

notes:
_____
_____
_____
_____
_____

Time	Monday	Tuesday	Wednesday	Thursday	Friday
6:00 AM					
7:00 AM					
8:00 AM					
9:00 AM					
10:00 AM					
11:00 AM					
12:00 NN					
1:00 PM					
2:00 PM					
3:00 PM					
4:00 PM					
5:00 PM					

notes:
_____
_____
_____
_____
_____

Time	Monday	Tuesday	Wednesday	Thursday	Friday
6:00 AM					
7:00 AM					
8:00 AM					
9:00 AM					
10:00 AM					
11:00 AM					
12:00 NN					
1:00 PM					
2:00 PM					
3:00 PM					
4:00 PM					
5:00 PM					

notes:
_____
_____
_____
_____
_____

Time	Monday	Tuesday	Wednesday	**Thursday**	Friday
6:00 AM					
7:00 AM					
8:00 AM					
9:00 AM					
10:00 AM					
11:00 AM					
12:00 NN					
1:00 PM					
2:00 PM					
3:00 PM					
4:00 PM					
5:00 PM					

notes:

Time	Monday	Tuesday	Wednesday	Thursday	Friday
6:00 AM					
7:00 AM					
8:00 AM					
9:00 AM					
10:00 AM					
11:00 AM					
12:00 NN					
1:00 PM					
2:00 PM					
3:00 PM					
4:00 PM					
5:00 PM					

notes:

Time	Monday	Tuesday	Wednesday	Thursday	Friday
6:00 AM					
7:00 AM					
8:00 AM					
9:00 AM					
10:00 AM					
11:00 AM					
12:00 NN					
1:00 PM					
2:00 PM					
3:00 PM					
4:00 PM					
5:00 PM					

notes:

Time	Monday	Tuesday	Wednesday	Thursday	Friday
6:00 AM					
7:00 AM					
8:00 AM					
9:00 AM					
10:00 AM					
11:00 AM					
12:00 NN					
1:00 PM					
2:00 PM					
3:00 PM					
4:00 PM					
5:00 PM					

notes:

Time	Monday	Tuesday	Wednesday	Thursday	Friday
6:00 AM					
7:00 AM					
8:00 AM					
9:00 AM					
10:00 AM					
11:00 AM					
12:00 NN					
1:00 PM					
2:00 PM					
3:00 PM					
4:00 PM					
5:00 PM					

notes:
_____
_____
_____
_____
_____

Time	Monday	Tuesday	Wednesday	**Thursday**	Friday
6:00 AM					
7:00 AM					
8:00 AM					
9:00 AM					
10:00 AM					
11:00 AM					
12:00 NN					
1:00 PM					
2:00 PM					
3:00 PM					
4:00 PM					
5:00 PM					

notes:
_____
_____
_____
_____
_____

Time	Monday	Tuesday	Wednesday	Thursday	Friday
6:00 AM					
7:00 AM					
8:00 AM					
9:00 AM					
10:00 AM					
11:00 AM					
12:00 NN					
1:00 PM					
2:00 PM					
3:00 PM					
4:00 PM					
5:00 PM					

notes:

Time	Monday	Tuesday	Wednesday	**Thursday**	Friday
6:00 AM					
7:00 AM					
8:00 AM					
9:00 AM					
10:00 AM					
11:00 AM					
12:00 NN					
1:00 PM					
2:00 PM					
3:00 PM					
4:00 PM					
5:00 PM					

notes:

Time	Monday	Tuesday	Wednesday	Thursday	Friday
6:00 AM					
7:00 AM					
8:00 AM					
9:00 AM					
10:00 AM					
11:00 AM					
12:00 NN					
1:00 PM					
2:00 PM					
3:00 PM					
4:00 PM					
5:00 PM					

notes:

Time	Monday	Tuesday	Wednesday	Thursday	Friday
6:00 AM					
7:00 AM					
8:00 AM					
9:00 AM					
10:00 AM					
11:00 AM					
12:00 NN					
1:00 PM					
2:00 PM					
3:00 PM					
4:00 PM					
5:00 PM					

notes:

Time	Monday	Tuesday	Wednesday	Thursday	Friday
6:00 AM					
7:00 AM					
8:00 AM					
9:00 AM					
10:00 AM					
11:00 AM					
12:00 NN					
1:00 PM					
2:00 PM					
3:00 PM					
4:00 PM					
5:00 PM					

notes:

Time	Monday	Tuesday	Wednesday	Thursday	Friday
6:00 AM					
7:00 AM					
8:00 AM					
9:00 AM					
10:00 AM					
11:00 AM					
12:00 NN					
1:00 PM					
2:00 PM					
3:00 PM					
4:00 PM					
5:00 PM					

notes:

Time	Monday	Tuesday	Wednesday	Thursday	Friday
6:00 AM					
7:00 AM					
8:00 AM					
9:00 AM					
10:00 AM					
11:00 AM					
12:00 NN					
1:00 PM					
2:00 PM					
3:00 PM					
4:00 PM					
5:00 PM					

notes:
_____
_____
_____
_____
_____

Time	Monday	Tuesday	Wednesday	Thursday	Friday
6:00 AM					
7:00 AM					
8:00 AM					
9:00 AM					
10:00 AM					
11:00 AM					
12:00 NN					
1:00 PM					
2:00 PM					
3:00 PM					
4:00 PM					
5:00 PM					

notes:

Time	Monday	Tuesday	Wednesday	Thursday	Friday
6:00 AM					
7:00 AM					
8:00 AM					
9:00 AM					
10:00 AM					
11:00 AM					
12:00 NN					
1:00 PM					
2:00 PM					
3:00 PM					
4:00 PM					
5:00 PM					

notes:

Time	Monday	Tuesday	Wednesday	Thursday	Friday
6:00 AM					
7:00 AM					
8:00 AM					
9:00 AM					
10:00 AM					
11:00 AM					
12:00 NN					
1:00 PM					
2:00 PM					
3:00 PM					
4:00 PM					
5:00 PM					

notes:

Time	Monday	Tuesday	Wednesday	Thursday	Friday
6:00 AM					
7:00 AM					
8:00 AM					
9:00 AM					
10:00 AM					
11:00 AM					
12:00 NN					
1:00 PM					
2:00 PM					
3:00 PM					
4:00 PM					
5:00 PM					

notes:

Time	Monday	Tuesday	Wednesday	**Thursday**	Friday
6:00 AM					
7:00 AM					
8:00 AM					
9:00 AM					
10:00 AM					
11:00 AM					
12:00 NN					
1:00 PM					
2:00 PM					
3:00 PM					
4:00 PM					
5:00 PM					

notes:

Time	Monday	Tuesday	Wednesday	**Thursday**	Friday
6:00 AM					
7:00 AM					
8:00 AM					
9:00 AM					
10:00 AM					
11:00 AM					
12:00 NN					
1:00 PM					
2:00 PM					
3:00 PM					
4:00 PM					
5:00 PM					

notes:

Time	Monday	Tuesday	Wednesday	Thursday	Friday
6:00 AM					
7:00 AM					
8:00 AM					
9:00 AM					
10:00 AM					
11:00 AM					
12:00 NN					
1:00 PM					
2:00 PM					
3:00 PM					
4:00 PM					
5:00 PM					

notes:
_____
_____
_____
_____
_____

Time	Monday	Tuesday	Wednesday	Thursday	Friday
6:00 AM					
7:00 AM					
8:00 AM					
9:00 AM					
10:00 AM					
11:00 AM					
12:00 NN					
1:00 PM					
2:00 PM					
3:00 PM					
4:00 PM					
5:00 PM					

notes:
_____
_____
_____
_____
_____

Time	Monday	Tuesday	Wednesday	**Thursday**	Friday
6:00 AM					
7:00 AM					
8:00 AM					
9:00 AM					
10:00 AM					
11:00 AM					
12:00 NN					
1:00 PM					
2:00 PM					
3:00 PM					
4:00 PM					
5:00 PM					

notes:
_____
_____
_____
_____
_____

Time	Monday	Tuesday	Wednesday	Thursday	Friday
6:00 AM					
7:00 AM					
8:00 AM					
9:00 AM					
10:00 AM					
11:00 AM					
12:00 NN					
1:00 PM					
2:00 PM					
3:00 PM					
4:00 PM					
5:00 PM					

notes:

_____

_____

_____

_____

Time	Monday	Tuesday	Wednesday	Thursday	Friday
6:00 AM					
7:00 AM					
8:00 AM					
9:00 AM					
10:00 AM					
11:00 AM					
12:00 NN					
1:00 PM					
2:00 PM					
3:00 PM					
4:00 PM					
5:00 PM					

notes:

Time	Monday	Tuesday	Wednesday	Thursday	Friday
6:00 AM					
7:00 AM					
8:00 AM					
9:00 AM					
10:00 AM					
11:00 AM					
12:00 NN					
1:00 PM					
2:00 PM					
3:00 PM					
4:00 PM					
5:00 PM					

notes:

Time	Monday	Tuesday	Wednesday	**Thursday**	Friday
6:00 AM					
7:00 AM					
8:00 AM					
9:00 AM					
10:00 AM					
11:00 AM					
12:00 NN					
1:00 PM					
2:00 PM					
3:00 PM					
4:00 PM					
5:00 PM					

notes:

Time	Monday	Tuesday	Wednesday	Thursday	Friday
6:00 AM					
7:00 AM					
8:00 AM					
9:00 AM					
10:00 AM					
11:00 AM					
12:00 NN					
1:00 PM					
2:00 PM					
3:00 PM					
4:00 PM					
5:00 PM					

notes:

Time	Monday	Tuesday	Wednesday	Thursday	Friday
6:00 AM					
7:00 AM					
8:00 AM					
9:00 AM					
10:00 AM					
11:00 AM					
12:00 NN					
1:00 PM					
2:00 PM					
3:00 PM					
4:00 PM					
5:00 PM					

notes:
_____
_____
_____
_____
_____

Time	Monday	Tuesday	Wednesday	Thursday	Friday
6:00 AM					
7:00 AM					
8:00 AM					
9:00 AM					
10:00 AM					
11:00 AM					
12:00 NN					
1:00 PM					
2:00 PM					
3:00 PM					
4:00 PM					
5:00 PM					

notes:

Time	Monday	Tuesday	Wednesday	Thursday	Friday
6:00 AM					
7:00 AM					
8:00 AM					
9:00 AM					
10:00 AM					
11:00 AM					
12:00 NN					
1:00 PM					
2:00 PM					
3:00 PM					
4:00 PM					
5:00 PM					

notes:

Time	Monday	Tuesday	Wednesday	Thursday	Friday
6:00 AM					
7:00 AM					
8:00 AM					
9:00 AM					
10:00 AM					
11:00 AM					
12:00 NN					
1:00 PM					
2:00 PM					
3:00 PM					
4:00 PM					
5:00 PM					

notes:

_____
_____
_____
_____
_____

Time	Monday	Tuesday	Wednesday	Thursday	Friday
6:00 AM					
7:00 AM					
8:00 AM					
9:00 AM					
10:00 AM					
11:00 AM					
12:00 NN					
1:00 PM					
2:00 PM					
3:00 PM					
4:00 PM					
5:00 PM					

notes:

Time	Monday	Tuesday	Wednesday	Thursday	Friday
6:00 AM					
7:00 AM					
8:00 AM					
9:00 AM					
10:00 AM					
11:00 AM					
12:00 NN					
1:00 PM					
2:00 PM					
3:00 PM					
4:00 PM					
5:00 PM					

notes:

Time	Monday	Tuesday	Wednesday	**Thursday**	Friday
6:00 AM					
7:00 AM					
8:00 AM					
9:00 AM					
10:00 AM					
11:00 AM					
12:00 NN					
1:00 PM					
2:00 PM					
3:00 PM					
4:00 PM					
5:00 PM					

notes:

Time	Monday	Tuesday	Wednesday	Thursday	Friday
6:00 AM					
7:00 AM					
8:00 AM					
9:00 AM					
10:00 AM					
11:00 AM					
12:00 NN					
1:00 PM					
2:00 PM					
3:00 PM					
4:00 PM					
5:00 PM					

notes:
_____
_____
_____
_____
_____

Time	Monday	Tuesday	Wednesday	Thursday	Friday
6:00 AM					
7:00 AM					
8:00 AM					
9:00 AM					
10:00 AM					
11:00 AM					
12:00 NN					
1:00 PM					
2:00 PM					
3:00 PM					
4:00 PM					
5:00 PM					

notes:

_____

_____

_____

_____

_____

Time	Monday	Tuesday	Wednesday	Thursday	Friday
6:00 AM					
7:00 AM					
8:00 AM					
9:00 AM					
10:00 AM					
11:00 AM					
12:00 NN					
1:00 PM					
2:00 PM					
3:00 PM					
4:00 PM					
5:00 PM					

notes:
_____
_____
_____
_____
_____

Time	Monday	Tuesday	Wednesday	**Thursday**	Friday
6:00 AM					
7:00 AM					
8:00 AM					
9:00 AM					
10:00 AM					
11:00 AM					
12:00 NN					
1:00 PM					
2:00 PM					
3:00 PM					
4:00 PM					
5:00 PM					

notes:

Time	Monday	Tuesday	Wednesday	Thursday	Friday
6:00 AM					
7:00 AM					
8:00 AM					
9:00 AM					
10:00 AM					
11:00 AM					
12:00 NN					
1:00 PM					
2:00 PM					
3:00 PM					
4:00 PM					
5:00 PM					

notes:

Time	Monday	Tuesday	Wednesday	Thursday	Friday
6:00 AM					
7:00 AM					
8:00 AM					
9:00 AM					
10:00 AM					
11:00 AM					
12:00 NN					
1:00 PM					
2:00 PM					
3:00 PM					
4:00 PM					
5:00 PM					

notes:

_____

_____

_____

_____

_____

Time	Monday	Tuesday	Wednesday	Thursday	Friday
6:00 AM					
7:00 AM					
8:00 AM					
9:00 AM					
10:00 AM					
11:00 AM					
12:00 NN					
1:00 PM					
2:00 PM					
3:00 PM					
4:00 PM					
5:00 PM					

notes:

Time	Monday	Tuesday	Wednesday	**Thursday**	Friday
6:00 AM					
7:00 AM					
8:00 AM					
9:00 AM					
10:00 AM					
11:00 AM					
12:00 NN					
1:00 PM					
2:00 PM					
3:00 PM					
4:00 PM					
5:00 PM					

notes:

Time	Monday	Tuesday	Wednesday	Thursday	Friday
6:00 AM					
7:00 AM					
8:00 AM					
9:00 AM					
10:00 AM					
11:00 AM					
12:00 NN					
1:00 PM					
2:00 PM					
3:00 PM					
4:00 PM					
5:00 PM					

notes:

_____

_____

_____

_____

_____

Time	Monday	Tuesday	Wednesday	Thursday	Friday
6:00 AM					
7:00 AM					
8:00 AM					
9:00 AM					
10:00 AM					
11:00 AM					
12:00 NN					
1:00 PM					
2:00 PM					
3:00 PM					
4:00 PM					
5:00 PM					

notes:
_____
_____
_____
_____
_____

Time	Monday	Tuesday	Wednesday	Thursday	Friday
6:00 AM					
7:00 AM					
8:00 AM					
9:00 AM					
10:00 AM					
11:00 AM					
12:00 NN					
1:00 PM					
2:00 PM					
3:00 PM					
4:00 PM					
5:00 PM					

notes:

Time	Monday	Tuesday	Wednesday	Thursday	Friday
6:00 AM					
7:00 AM					
8:00 AM					
9:00 AM					
10:00 AM					
11:00 AM					
12:00 NN					
1:00 PM					
2:00 PM					
3:00 PM					
4:00 PM					
5:00 PM					

notes:

Time	Monday	Tuesday	Wednesday	Thursday	Friday
6:00 AM					
7:00 AM					
8:00 AM					
9:00 AM					
10:00 AM					
11:00 AM					
12:00 NN					
1:00 PM					
2:00 PM					
3:00 PM					
4:00 PM					
5:00 PM					

notes:
_____
_____
_____
_____
_____

www.ingramcontent.com/pod-product-compliance
Lightning Source LLC
Chambersburg PA
CBHW080737250626
47170CB00010B/2861